Bats

Nocturnal Flyers

Rebecca Rissman

Heinemann
LIBRARY
Chicago, Illinois

Edited by Brynn Baker, Clare Lewis, and Helen Cox Cannons
Designed by Kyle Grenz and Tim Bond
Picture research by Tracy Cummins
Production by Helen McCreath
Originated by Capstone Global Library Ltd
Printed and bound in China by Leo Paper Group

18 17 16 15 14
10 9 8 7 6 5 4 3 2 1

Library of Congress Cataloging-in-Publication Data

ISBN 978-1-4846-0309-3 (hardcover)
ISBN 978-1-4846-0315-4 (paperback)
ISBN 978-1-4846-0327-7 (eBook PDF)

Acknowledgments
We would like to thank the following for permission to reproduce photographs: Ardea: © Yves Bilat, 6, 23f; FLPA: Christian Ziegler/Minden Pictures, 11, Claus Meyer/Minden Pictures, 19, Derek Middleton, 7 mouse, Emanuele Biggi, 9, 23h, Hugh Clark, 21, front cover, Hugh Lansdown, 17, 23e, Imagebroker, 7 owl, Michael Durham/Minden Pictures 13, 18, 22, back cover, Michael Mayer, 20, Michel Rauch/Biosphoto, 4, 10, 23d, Roger Tidman, 16, 23c; Getty Images Auscape/UIG, 12, 23b, Fred Bruemmer, 15, James Hager, 5, Les Stocker, 14; Shutterstock: Andrew Astbury, 7 fox, Piotr Krzeslak, 7 hedgehog

Every effort has been made to contact copyright holders of material reproduced in this book. Any omissions will be rectified in subsequent printings if notice is given to the publisher.

All the Internet addresses (URLs) given in this book were valid at the time of going to press. However, due to the dynamic nature of the Internet, some addresses may have changed, or sites may have changed or ceased to exist since publication. While the author and publisher regret any inconvenience this may cause readers, no responsibility for any such changes can be accepted by either the author or the publisher.

Contents

What Is a Bat?

A bat is a small, flying **mammal**. It has large ears, small eyes, and sharp teeth.

Bats have long arms attached to their leathery wings for support.

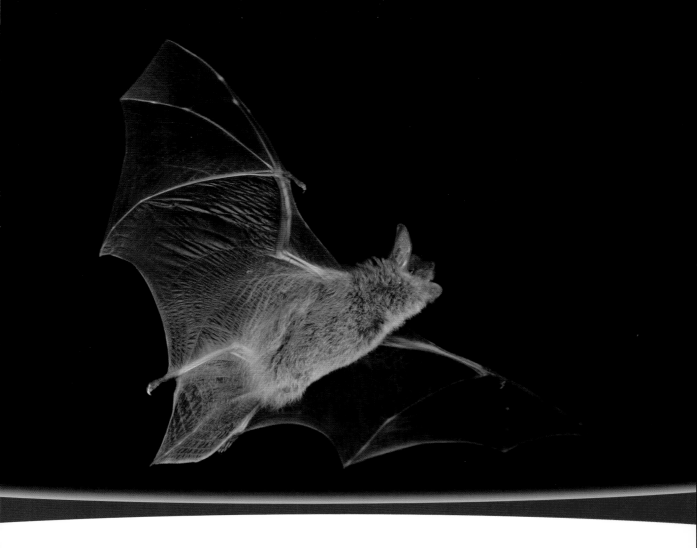

Bats are rarely seen during the day. This is because they are **nocturnal**.

What Does Nocturnal Mean?

Nocturnal means awake during the night.

Animals that are nocturnal sleep during the day.

Many animals are nocturnal.

Foxes, owls, hedgehogs, and mice are nocturnal.

Where Do Bats Live?

Bats live on every **continent** except for Antarctica.

They live in groups called colonies.

Bats spend days sleeping in dark, quiet places called **roosts**.

Roosts can be found in caves, holes in trees, and even in some attics!

What Do Bats Eat?

Different types of bats eat different foods.

Most bats eat small insects, such as moths, beetles, and flies.

Many bats eat pests, such as mosquitos. Some bats eat fruit.

Some bats even drink the blood of other animals!

How Do Bats Find Prey?

Most bats look for food at night when it is dark outside.

Some bats use **echolocation** to find food to eat.

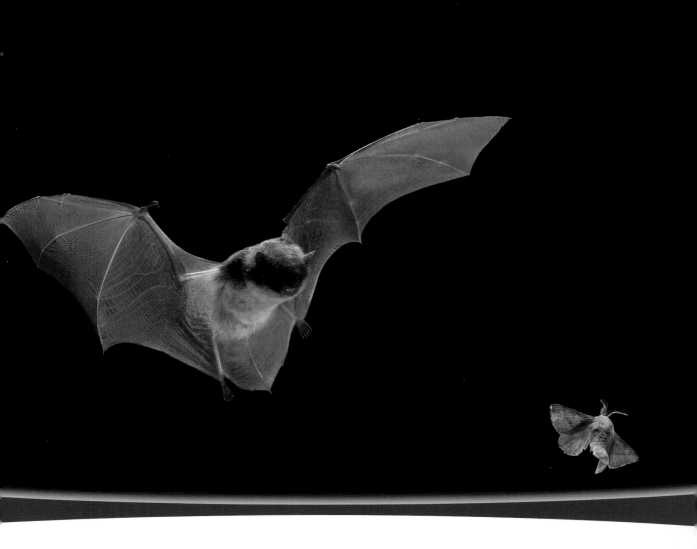

Bats make noises and listen for echoes.

Their sensitive ears tell them where food can be found.

What Are Bat Babies Like?

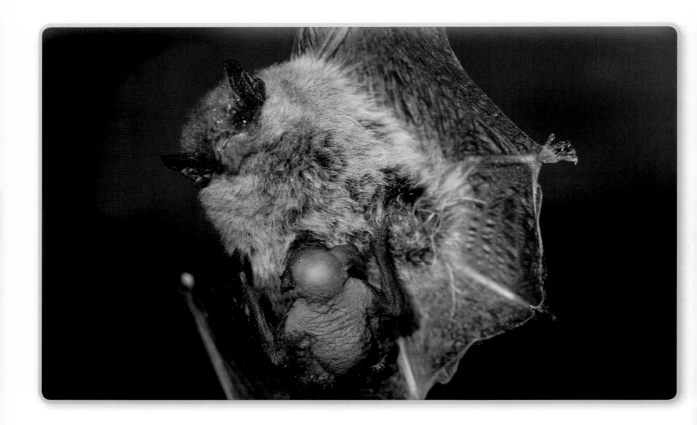

Each year, female bats give birth to one or two babies called pups.

The pups are hairless and very small.

Female bats care for their pups for about one month.

Then the young bats fly off by themselves.

Where Do Bats Go in Winter?

Many bats **hibernate** during winter.

They sleep in a safe, warm place
until spring.

Other bats **migrate**.

They fly to warmer places during winter and return to their homes every spring.

How Can You Spot Bats?

Bats are most active one or two hours after the Sun sets.

Some of the most common places bats live are in caves or tree hollows.

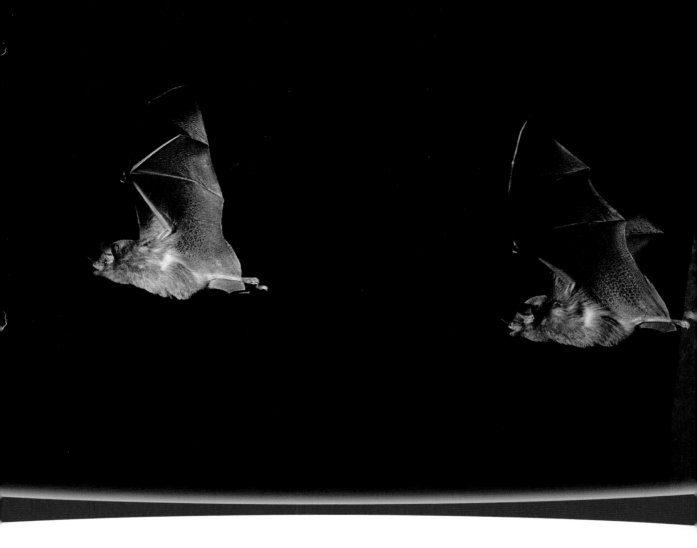

Bats do not fly in smooth lines like most birds. Bats fly in jerky zigzags.

Watch the skies carefully for small animals making twists and turns.

How Can You Help Bats?

Avoid using sprays to poison pests.

They make it hard for bats to find food.

Never touch bats. Some bats carry diseases that can make you ill.

If you see a bat, tell a trusted adult.

Bat Body Map

Picture Glossary

 **continent** one of seven huge areas of land on Earth

 echolocation the use of sound vibrations for navigation

 **hibernate** to spend the winter in a deep sleep

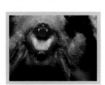 **mammal** warm-blooded animal that has a back-bone, hair or fur, and gives birth to live babies that feed on milk from the mother

 **migrate** when an animal moves from one area to another because of the seasons

 **nocturnal** awake at night and asleep during the day

 **roost** quiet, dark place bats gather and sleep

Find Out More

Books

Stewart, Melissa. *How Do Bats Fly in the Dark?* Tell Me Why, Tell Me How. New York: Marshall Cavendish Benchmark, 2009.

Whitehouse, Patricia. *Bats.* What's Awake? Chicago: Heinemann Library, 2010.

Websites

Learn more about bat facts at:
http://defenders.org/bats/bats

Discover more about bat conservation and research at:
www.flybynightinc.org

Index